Sneakers! Sneakers!

Written by Angela Shelf Medearis
Illustrated by David Gaadt

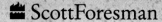
ScottForesman
A Division of HarperCollins*Publishers*

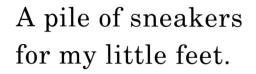

A pile of sneakers
for my little feet.

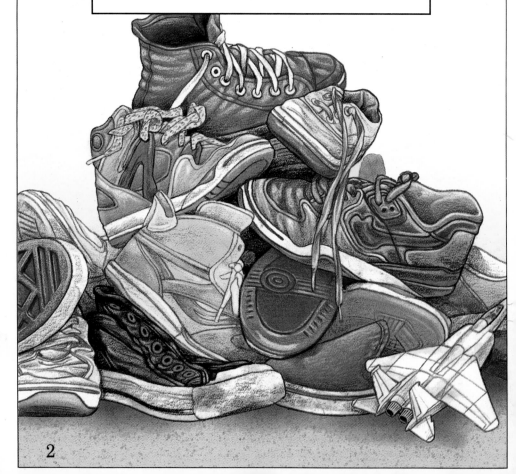

2

Black sneakers
with high tops and laces.

3

Red sneakers
for sports and races.

4

Green sneakers
pumped full of air.

Gold sneakers
like rock stars wear.

White sneakers
to skip down the street.

I need so many sneakers
for my little feet.